EXECUTIVES HAVE ADHD

STAY PASSIONATE

EXECUTIVES
HAVE ADHD

THE ART OF THE STORY

Marc LeShay

ISBN: 0692772731
ISBN 13: 9780692772737

For all the wonderful mentors who patiently taught me how to be a professional.
For my amazing students, with whom the concepts in this book took form.
For Veronica, who tirelessly worked with and inspired me to complete this book.
And for Brenda and Rebecca, who make me who I am.

CONTENTS

PREFACE

IF I CAN DO IT, ANYONE CAN

When I was twenty-three years old, I was an analyst at the corporate offices of one of the world's largest banks. As part of my annual review, I was asked to accompany my entire team to a writing workshop. The assignment seemed simple enough. So, I did as I was asked and attended the writing class from Monday to Thursday, then wrote an essay on Friday. At the time, I had no idea of the profound impact that week would have on my career and me.

One week later, the workshop instructor came to our office to provide one-on-one feedback on our essays. I went about my daily business but was unable to fully focus due to the anticipation. I couldn't wait to hear how well I did. I never felt like I was a great writer, but I had taken Advanced Placement English in high school and the mandatory two semesters of writing at New York University. Needless to say, I was feeling pretty good about the essay I had prepared.

Finally, it was my turn. I entered the conference room, sat down, and said, "So, how did I do?"

The instructor's response is one I will never forget: She looked me in the eye and replied, "You may be the worst writer I've ever had." Seeing how she had some years on her, this was quite a declaration. It was like being punched in the gut. Despite spending half an hour with the instructor, I can't recall a single word she said after that. Those six words just rattled around in my head like a song that I couldn't stop singing to myself. *The worst writer I've ever had.*

For the next four years, those words haunted me, and I experienced minor anxiety attacks every time I had to write anything, even a simple e-mail. To compensate, I began to use PowerPoint presentations, full of beautiful illustrations and graphics, relying on simple phraseology—anything to avoid any form of narrative. Over time, I became better and better at presentations and was able to hide my writing deficiency. As I moved up the corporate ladder, I was able to rely on staff to take on the writing burdens, with me summarizing their prose in beautiful presentations. Problem solved.

Ultimately, however, I was unable to hide from myself. This writing thing gnawed at me and eroded my confidence. At age twenty-seven, I decided enough was enough and made it my mission to overcome this personal hurdle. I reached out to a few trusted peers, told them about my writing woes, and requested their assistance. Their unanimous advice: "Keep it simple." I owe a tremendous debt to those generous mentors.

Today, executives hail my communication skills, often paying me ridiculous fees to teach their staffs how to write an effective story. I even teach at a top business school. It was a lot of work, but with a lot of help, I learned how to write and develop compelling executive stories. It was a long but incredibly rewarding journey.

This book is the sum of that journey.

INTRODUCTION

THE BEST STORY WINS

Contrary to years of societal programming that each of us has received, it's not the smartest, funniest, best-looking, or (fill in the blank) person who wins. In the boardroom, as in life, it is the person with the best story who claims victory.

But I jump ahead. Let's first look at how business organizations are composed. At the staff and midlevel managerial levels, we have the "doers." On the other end, we have the "thinkers," who are invited to join the executive ranks as vice president and higher. *Thought leadership* is a combination of creativity, intellect, and understanding that our solutions have to solve real problems that will impact the business's values. Storytelling is how you demonstrate to your executives that you are a thought leader and have the ability to enroll others in your vision. If you can't master storytelling, particularly to your executives, you'll find that your career stagnates at the mid-management level.

So, what is "the best story"? How do we know which is best, and more importantly, how do we craft and tell that story? This book is dedicated to answering these central questions. The process begins by accepting these two concepts:

1) We have to let go of academic tenets that have been deeply ingrained in us during our formative years.

2) We have to accept that responsibility for communication resides with the sender, not the receiver.

From the time we're five or six years old, schools teach us how to write beautiful narratives. Prose that is formulaically drawn out, detailed, colorful, and full of imagery. In fact, there are classes dedicated to interpreting and developing each of these qualities to ensure we become not only proficient but also comfortable crafting stories with these ingredients. I am not diminishing the value of such training. The ability to develop stories in this fashion is responsible for beautiful literary works of art. However, the boardroom is not about literary works of art, nor about entertainment (well, it is a little); it is about short, crisp, undeniably clear communication.

Executives, having to focus on several issues at one time, see the world through a unique lens. They have very short attention spans—in fact, they have ADHD (attention deficit hyperactivity disorder). You don't have the luxury of fifty pages for narrative exposition. Often, you don't get even one. Your job is to get directly to the point and to clearly present that point in crystal clarity, in a manner that deeply resonates with your audience—and you have approximately five minutes or less to grab the listeners' attention, dazzle them, and sell your idea. The person who can do this best wins. To achieve this, we have to shed years of ingrained traditional academic writing. To be successful with an executive audience, you must harness and focus your ideas into executive points.

But this is only half the challenge. We have to take responsibility for the entire dialogue. I often have people tell me, "That won't work here," or "So-and-so doesn't understand the issues/problems, and so forth."

My response is consistent and direct: "Then you didn't tell the right story." In communication, the problem always resides with the sender, not the receiver. The sooner we accept this, the sooner we can correct our messaging and become effective executive storytellers.

So, what is a good story? It possesses the following:

- It is rooted in a value proposition that resonates with your executive team.

- It solves a real problem.

- It is timely.

- It is supported by detailed analysis but presented in an easily digestible summary form.

- It communicates what the executives need to hear, and only what they need to hear.

- It has a seamless and natural flow.

- It is visually appealing and attractive.

- All this and much more.

Easy, right? Unfortunately, as we emerge from college and graduate school to enter the business world, we are often ill-equipped to be successful storytellers. It will take some time to let go of our academic foundation and learn how to skillfully rotate the prism to see problems from various perspectives and select the most impactful story lines, to synthesize chaos into clarity, to visualize and present our thoughts in powerful ways. My goal with this book is not only to help you learn how to do this, but also to provide you with the tools to make you highly proficient and skilled in the process.

This book will walk you through the entire arc of how to craft and tell a compelling corporate story to all levels of executives, from inception to final presentation.

CHAPTER 1

STORY CONCEPT
Preview

B efore you commit to an action plan, ask yourself one basic
question:

"What is the value of my idea?"

In your analysis, consider these things:

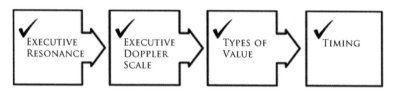

Keys to success:

1. Determine if your story will resonate with executives.
   First, establish perspective and the value proposition.

   a. Are you looking at the environment through your
      eyes or the eyes of your audience and your executive
      team?

b. Does your idea hold executive resonance? Will this idea generate revenue, reduce cost, protect the brand, or ensure compliance?

If no, stop right here.
If yes, proceed.

2. Use the Executive Doppler Scale (discussed in this chapter) to measure the degrees of separation between your idea and the above outcome.

3. Determine what type of values your solution will deliver: hard or soft values?

4. Since timing is everything, ask yourself, "Is this the right time for my idea?"

Putting the above together, we form "The Value Chain." All four of these areas need to be assessed to determine whether or not to proceed and tell your story.

Story Concept

Before you write a single sentence, ask yourself two basic questions:

1. What is the problem I am trying to solve?

2. Is there value to my story?

The greatest challenge in answering these questions is our natural tendency to see and interpret the world through our own eyes. After all, we are all bound by our experiences. They shape our perspective on life.

Once, a member of my staff came into my office exclaiming that we needed to purchase new computer hardware. When I asked why, he told me that the existing technology failed every night and he had to wake up at 2:00 a.m. to manually restart the equipment. He was incredibly frustrated and informed me that, for more than a year, he had been trying to get someone to approve new hardware.

I told him, "I don't care if the servers fail every night; I don't have to wake up." He then explained, "Every time the servers go down, we cannot take online orders."

I was certainly interested and explained to him that in his approach he was "burying the lead" by not giving me the most crucial and critical information first. He had been having trouble convincing people they needed new equipment because he was telling *his* story of being woken up in the wee hours, not the story (unable to take orders) that *his executives* cared about.

He and I put together a quick summary presentation and had new hardware approved that week.

As a storyteller, this becomes a central challenge for you. Consider the problem you are trying to solve. Is it a problem that an executive cares about?

1. Executive Resonance

To determine whether or not your executives will care about your story, consider the value delivered by solving this problem. Look beyond your horizon and put yourself in the mind of an executive; turn the prism and see the world through his or her lens. When you do this, you'll see a very simple yet vibrant world, one where four primary values (story themes) emerge:

1. Generating revenue (and profit)

2. Reducing or deferring cost

3. Protecting the brand

4. Achieving compliance (corporate and/or regulatory)—which could equate to staying out of jail

Regardless of your personal interpretation of the problem and the value of your story, it has to fit into one of these four themes. This can sometimes feel disingenuous and create personal conflict. So, I want to be clear: I am not suggesting you lie or deceive your audience. Rather, I'm simply spotlighting the reality that your story has to revolve around one of these four themes, or it may not be sellable to an executive audience.

There is a scene in the movie *Temple Grandin* where Grandin wants to sell a group of meat-packers on a new method for herding cattle to the slaughterhouse. In her proposed solution, the cattle ranchers would have to invest in new fencing and a conveyer-belt system to transport the cows to their execution.

While she readily accepts the need to slaughter cows for their meat, Grandin's personal view or value for the proposed solution is that she fundamentally believes that we, as a modern civilized society, have the ability to kill the cows more humanely.

WILL THIS IDEA GENERATE REVENUE, REDUCE COSTS, PROTECT THE BRAND, OR ENSURE COMPLIANCE?

Recognizing that sentimentality will not sell to her audience, Grandin tells her story in terms that will resonate with cattle ranchers: She makes two central arguments:

1. They can reduce costs, as this new system does not require any ranchers, and

2. They can increase profits with an improved product, since not only will fewer cows die in the process, but also they will not even be agitated, so they will yield higher-quality meat for consumers.

Ultimately, the ranchers agree to her proposal, which goes on to revolutionize the cattle-handling industry. The only reason Temple Grandin could sell her story was because she turned the prism and selected values that were consistent with those of her audience rather than her personal views.

While it's not possible to provide values for every type of company, below are three types of organizations and some pointers for determining value resonance.

1. **Private Equity**. If a private equity firm owns your organization, it views the company as an investment. As such, the equity firm's needs are simple: It needs to grow the company value so it can sell the business for more than what was paid—ideally, seven to ten times as much. So, your stories should center on this value proposition.

2. **Public**. Public companies are required to post annual reports. These documents clearly outline the goals of the C-level executives (the chief executive officer, chief operating officer, chief financial officer and other titles starting with "chief") and the board of directors. They will also provide insight into the organization's current values and financial situation. Keep in mind that using their language in your presentation is a really powerful way to connect to your audience.

3. **Large Private**. Perhaps the trickiest, these organizations can have many layers without the benefit of published documents. However, you should consider meeting minutes, town halls, speeches, and marketing materials as good sources of information. Also, don't be shy. If you don't know what the company's executives value and what their future growth strategies are, ask.

Regardless of the type of organization you work for, simply asking leadership questions about values and the current state of the organization will give you a better picture of what your executives are facing. Being aware of the challenges and opportunities within your company is your job—so don't be afraid to ask!

2. The Executive Doppler Scale

To recap, start the process by asking yourself, "Does the punch line of my story result in any of the above executive themes?" If the answer is no, stop right there.

If the answer is yes, next ask, "How many degrees of separation is my story from these goals?" I refer to this as the *Executive Doppler Scale*. The way this works is simple. If the story directly yields a reduction in cost, that's one degree of separation. However, if what you're suggesting creates efficiency that enables a team to become more productive, which then makes another team more productive, thus allowing them to reduce staff levels—well, that's three degrees.

Essentially, as you travel along each ring of the *Executive Doppler Scale*, your story becomes a string of logic that says, "If this, then if this, then if this . . . then we achieve value." Each degree of separation creates uncertainty in achieving the end result. Thus, the further out your story falls on the *Executive Doppler Scale*, the higher the risk of not achieving that goal. As such, my rule of thumb is anything more than three degrees of separation loses enough credibility to send the idea into the circular file—the trash can.

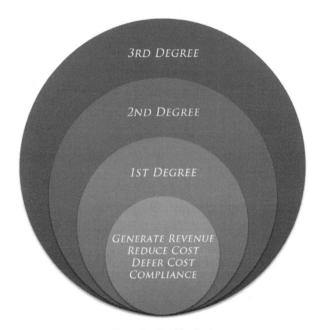

Executive Doppler Scale

Say you want to increase sales dollars. A first- degree solution would be a new direct-to-consumer sales system to directly drive revenue. A second-degree solution would be a sales system that the sales team uses to make sales and drive revenue. A third-degree solution would be to implement a tool that feeds into the existing sales support system used by the sales team when selling to customers to drive revenue. As you can see, the further out you get from the executive value, the more convoluted and diluted it becomes.

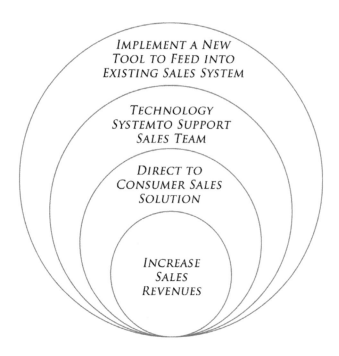

3. Hard Versus Soft Values

Armed with a strong theme with minimal degrees of separation, your story appears to have value. Yet not all value is created equal. Particularly in today's economy, executives are seeking *hard* values. These are benefits that are tangible and empirically quantifiable. For example, implementing a project that reduces manufacturing costs by $1 million is a hard value. Alternatively, implementing a project that creates efficiencies that cannot be measured but are agreed to be real are considered soft values. Frequently, customer-service teams face these challenges. While everyone will agree that better customer service will yield happier customers, and that happier customers purchase more products, the fact that it's nearly impossible to empirically relate the proposed activities can make a project difficult to sell. Of course, this all depends on the company and its values. The above customer-service challenge may be easier to sell at Nordstrom than at Macy's.

As a rule, it is easier to sell hard value than soft value. That doesn't mean soft value cannot be sold. It can and is every day. Your role as a storyteller is just a bit more complex with soft value. Typically, in addition to the four primary executive themes, you will need to weave in additional elements. One effective way to achieve this is to leverage the words of the executives themselves. For example, if the executive team presented materials on the need to reduce customer churn, use its words in justifying your customer-service initiative.

TURN THE PRISM AND SEE THE WORLD THROUGH THEIR LENS.

A cautionary note: Be sure to recognize the difference between your executives *espoused values* and *values in practice.* As with all of us, executives are prone to their version of cognitive dissonance, where they say one thing (espoused values) but actually do another (values in practice). If you're going to leverage your executives' words in your argument, consider the source. How do you do this? Since this is not a book on culture and leadership, I'll simplify this narrative: Look around your environment and take notice of what type of behavior is exemplified and *rewarded* by your leadership team.

4. Timing Is Everything

As in life, the timing of your story is critical. Executives typically have more good ideas than they can implement. To be arbiters of the analysis, they look at everything we've discussed: resonance with their four themes, the Executive Doppler Scale, hard versus soft values, and the final element: timing.

To evaluate whether the timing is right, consider these questions:

1. Does my story address a critical issue facing the company?

2. What is the likelihood my story will achieve the proposed benefits?

3. What is the impact of their not accepting my story?

For example, your company just completed a very successful compliance audit. Your story proposes implementing some systems that will generate even greater efficiencies throughout the compliance process. While your story is a good one, sound from all angles, it may not be considered critical since the existing solutions are yielding success. Conversely, if the company just received a negative audit, the exact same proposal may be easily sold.

Never throw away a good story. Hold on to it. You never know when timing will turn in your favor. Many years ago, I remember working at a major studio. One day, I received a phone call from the chief information officer (CIO). A website had been hacked so that every time someone clicked on an image, a porn site popped up. As part of my investigation, I spoke with the IT security team. Team members informed me that, to prevent such a cyber-attack, they had tried to purchase some new technology—which the CIO had denied just a couple of months prior to the incident. I asked if they still had the proposal, which they did. I walked up to the CIO's office and presented it to him. I'm not exaggerating: I put the proposal on his desk and said this will dramatically reduce the risk of future similar attacks. He asked how much. I told him $50,000. He didn't even read the proposal. He just said, "Go buy two."

Timing is everything!

Chapter Summary

Before you invest in developing your story, ask yourself, "Is there value to my story?" To answer that question, consider the following:

- Turn the prism and craft your message into one that will resonate with an executive. Does your story yield one of the four primary themes?
  1. Generating revenue (and profit)
  2. Reducing or deferring cost
  3. Protecting the brand
  4. Achieving compliance (corporate and/or regulatory)

- Use the Executive Doppler Scale to determine your degrees of separation from the four primary themes. Remain within three degrees.

- Consider whether your story yields hard or soft values. Hard values are easier to sell, but soft values can be sold with additional thought and development.

- Timing is everything. In evaluating whether or not it's a good time for your story, ask yourself a few key questions:
  1. Does my story address a critical issue facing the company?
  2. What is the likelihood the story achieves the proposed benefits?
  3. What is the impact of their not accepting my story?

- Never throw away a good story. Events can shift, creating a more favorable time in the future.

CHAPTER 2

STORY OUTLINE
Preview

O nce you've established a clear value statement, you're ready to craft your story outline.

"What information and flow is required to tell an impactful story?"

Through this process, remain focused on the following:

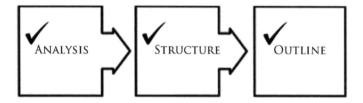

Keys to success:

1. Perform a thorough story analysis. Be sure to include the following:

   A. Current state
   B. Future state

    C. Gaps and barriers

    D. Roadmap

    E. Sustainability

2. Adhere to the LeShay Executive 4x4

3. Story Outline Best Practices

    A. Don't beat around the bush. Instead, send your message right up front. Executives are top-down thinkers and will easily follow this organization.

    B. Avoid compound story lines. Remain focused on only one message. Your story is not a soap opera.

    C. Simple is always better. Follow an easy to follow A=B, B=C, C=D, and A=D progression (a.k.a. "the slow seduction").

    D. Ensure that your message is clear.

If you've done the work to carefully craft your story as outlined above, you should find your audience reaching your conclusions.

Story Outline

Now that you've determined that there's value to your story, the next step is generating your story outline and flow.

1. The Story Analysis

There are hundreds of thoughts on, and approaches to, developing an impactful story. Below is one "flow" that I have used and has proven tried and true.

A. Current State

Where is the company now? As we'll discuss throughout the book, be sure that this analysis is developed from the executives' perspectives. As we described in chapter 1, it's not important to an executive that the "current state" is that equipment crashes every night. What the executive cares about is that, currently, the company has a significant risk of losing revenue due to faulty equipment.

Also, be sure your current-state assessment adheres to a few rules:

1. Make your analysis holistic. People, process, and technology all need to be considered.

2. Make sure you validate your analysis. More times than not, documentation is not reality, especially when it comes to processes. To validate your processes, I recommend you "walk the floor"—go and

see first-hand what is really happening. Over time, people adapt processes and create undocumented "work-arounds." It's critical to see what's really going on, especially in companies where tribal knowledge is predominant (which, in my experience, is the majority of companies).

3. Stay focused. It's easy to get distracted and/or expand your scope. Remain on target.

B. Future State

What is your vision for how the world should look? Again, be sure your vision includes people, processes, and technology. And again, be sure to consider your vision in terms that will resonate with an executive.

C. Gaps and Barriers

There are certain to be obstacles that lie in the path between your current and future states. Document these and then distill them to the most salient points for your executives. A rule of thumb is to share *only* obstacles that require their attention. If the gaps or barriers can be overcome at levels below the executives, then don't bother them with these.

In your analysis, consider a wide spectrum of obstacles, but limit your executives to the following:

- Cost constraints

- Time constraints

- Legal concerns

- Paradigm changes (such as outsourcing currently performed work)

- Concerns about Intellectual property/rights

- "Cultural" barriers or changes (including political realities)

D. Roadmap

Careful consideration has to be paid to how you propose to overcome the gaps and deliver your vision. You need to consider how to break your effort into logical segments and sequence all of this to drive successful implementation. As this is not a project management book, I'm going to assume you know how to do this.

What I want to focus on is making sure that this part of your story, the roadmap, doesn't get overly complicated. As always, keep in mind that executives have ADHD and like things to be stupidly simple. I don't care how complex and/or broad your project; your job is to come up with a very simple story to explain how you're going to execute your vision. To this end, I highly suggest leveraging graphics and, if necessary, very simple animations. Below are a couple of real-life examples of illustrations.

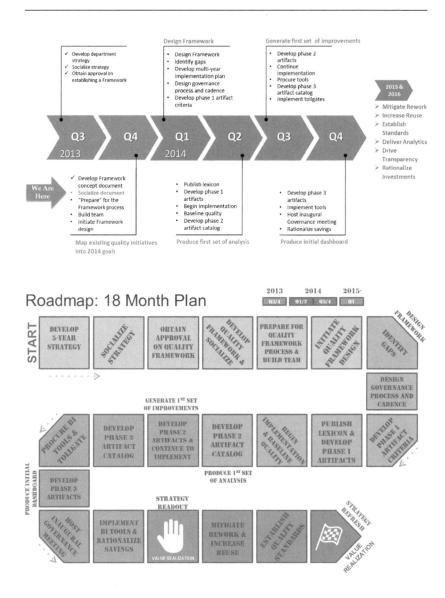

E. Sustainability

If you purchased a classic car and spent $60,000 to restore it to mint condition, would you then just leave it on the front yard and let fate take its course? Of course not. Yet so many companies fail to consider the ongoing requirements to maintain their programs, projects, and assets.

Case in point: I once worked with a Fortune 100 entertainment company on a project to review and implement enhancements to all its business-critical systems to increase system availability to 99.99 percent uptime. I entered the project in the final stages, after nearly $7 million had been spent. My assignment was to get the program wrapped up and delivered. After reviewing the program, I noticed there was no analysis or plan in place to sustain the purchased enhancements and ensure performance could be maintained at 99.99 percent. So, I raised this to the leadership team, which told me to not worry about it and just finish the project. I pulled my sponsor aside and told him that, within two years, this would all revert back, probably to lower levels than before.

Fast forward. I'm driving and receive a call from my client: "You remember when you said we'd be right back where we started in two years? Well, we're right on schedule. Can you come in and help?" So, I returned to perform the same job again but this time added controls to ensure the gains could be sustained across time.

When assessing your sustainability plan, consider the following two types of controls:

1. *Project controls* to ensure the project is advancing on budget, on time, and on target. Also, those controls would ensure that the project objectives are actually met and your stakeholders are satisfied.

2. *Operational controls* to ensure that the investment is protected and the gains are sustained over time.

The previous example of failing to protect the attained 99.99 percent uptime is an example where operational controls were not defined, developed, and managed.

BE SURE THAT THIS ANALYSIS IS DEVELOPED FROM THE PERSPECTIVE OF THE EXECUTIVES.

Controls, like your current and future states, should also be holistic. When developing your controls, consider the people, processes, and technologies related to project and operational aspects. There are literally hundreds of possible well-established controls that you can find with a simple Google search. Below are just a few examples.

People
- Staff changes, training, augmentation, etc.
- Business partnerships and maintenance contracts
- Reward systems

Processes
- Project governance processes (including tollgates – meetings to review progress, verify alignment, and achieve appropriate approvals *before* advancing to the next stage)
- Feedback systems from customer and all other stakeholders
- Hiring practices
- Business, project, and technology standards

Technology
- Executive and staff dashboards
- Maintenance windows

- Technology management systems (monitor technology and provide alerts during specific conditions—similar to a thermostat)

2. The LeShay Executive 4x4

Outlining your story is a lot of work. But the real work is just beginning because now you have to compile all the information and figure out how to distill and format it for your executives.

For this, I recommend the simple and formulaic story line found below. The LeShay Executive 4x4 draws on my experience both as a senior level executive as well as my nearly thirty years presenting to senior level executives. It doesn't have to be followed literally, but these elements have to be prominent and clearly included. If an executive has to hunt for this information, he or she will just stop listening to the story or reading it.

21

As we've said, executives are busy. They want you to cut to the chase. But they also want and need basic information to make an educated decision.

STARTING POINT: What problem are you trying to solve?
You should be able to distill the problem into a single, simple sentence. If you have to spend a lot of time explaining your problem statement, you're on the wrong path and need to reevaluate.

Also, be sure your problem statement is truly hitting the root cause and is not just a symptom. As trivial as this seems, you would be surprised at how many millions of dollars large corporations spend on initiatives that have no clear problem statement.

YOUR JOB IS TO COME UP WITH A VERY SIMPLE STORY TO EXPLAIN HOW YOU'RE GOING TO EXECUTE YOUR VISION.

Case in point: I have a Fortune 100 client that recently paid a consulting firm to develop a strategy document. I was hired to review the document and provide additional insights as well as an implementation roadmap. To my surprise, when I asked what problem my client was trying to address, the room went silent. After spending several hundred thousand dollars to develop a strategy, nobody in the room could even tell me what they were trying to achieve. Needless to say, this is unproductive and, had the document made it to the C-level executive team, it would have been quickly dismissed. Luckily, we rectified the oversight—which as a matter of importance significantly changed the strategy document—and submitted it to the executive team, which approved it.

Once you've defined the problem you're trying to solve, outline your story with the four pieces of information that matter to your audience, the executives.

1. **What will you do?**
   Assuming you grabbed the executives' attention with your problem statement, you now need to very quickly provide an impactful solution. Start by explaining specifically what it is you're planning to do. One of the biggest mistakes people make here is to "bury" their solution below a ton of foundational stuff such as long introductions that reiterate a lot of information the audience is keenly aware of. For example, you don't need to remind the senior executive team when the company was founded, its mission, and so forth. Get straight to the point.

2. **When will you do this?**
   Executives don't have the attention span to listen to and follow a multiphased timeline with various deliverables, etc. So, pay attention to two things: 1) keep your plan simple, and 2) show them a pretty picture (like the ones illustrated earlier in this chapter). Executives love shiny things and pretty pictures. Generate a very simple timeline that clearly articulates the phased approach, timing, and major deliverables. Lastly, when listing your deliverables, DO NOT list document names; list the results. In other words, they don't care about the "what" (the document); they care about the "so what" (the result).

3. **How much will it cost?**

I once sat in an investor meeting with an entrepreneur presenting to a board of executives/investors, and he said—and I quote—"I'm not going to show you a bunch of fancy financials because we all know they're useless." Buzzzzz, wrong thing to say!

Executives *always* want to know the cost. More specifically, they want to know the total cost of ownership. Don't go into a meeting with an executive with discrete costs and expect to have a conversation beyond "Get out!" You need to do your homework and prepare a cost analysis that takes into consideration the total cost of ownership, including hardware, software, licensing, maintenance, labor, outside services, training, implementation, etc.

Also, depending on your organization, executives will very likely want to see some type of return on investment (ROI) analysis. There are several variations on this analysis, and your company probably prefers one to another. Educate yourself on what format and level of ROI analysis is required and how to perform that analysis. If you don't know how to perform the analysis, here are a few options:

- Get a previous ROI analysis document and see if you can re-create it.

- Get help from your financial personnel. They are almost always willing to help "crunch" your numbers and ensure your analysis is solidly developed.

- Do some research online to understand ROI analysis and the various tools or techniques used.

- Enroll in a finance class at a local community college, online university, etc. This solution takes the most time.

Keeping with the overarching theme of this book, you should make your financial analysis simple: Start with the top-level numbers and drill down into the detail as directed by the executives. In other words, do your due diligence and be prepared to go delve into all the nitty-gritty details, but don't overwhelm your executives with this up front. Distill your analysis into a crisp top-down story and navigate your executives only as far down as they want to go.

4. **What value will the effort return?**
   So, what is it that you're going to deliver to your executives? If you recall, in chapter 1 we discussed the four things that an executive cares about:

1. You're going to generate revenue.

2. You're going to reduce or defer cost.

3. You're going to protect or enhance the company's brand.

4. You're going to keep the executives out of jail.

These are your only choices. Your story has to culminate in one of these four value statements, or you're going to lose your executives' attention. Again, keep in mind the Executive Doppler Scale (also from chapter 1). The further out from the center your solution is, the less likely it is that you'll succeed. Again, anything beyond the third degree is doomed for failure.

3. Story Outline Best Practices

A. Don't beat around the bush.

Executives have very little patience. Your message has to be concise and to the point. You have literally one minute to capture their attention, or they'll move on. Remember this while preparing your story outline.

B. Avoid compound story lines.

They may be great for motion pictures, but compound story lines don't work in the boardroom. It's hard enough to get your ADHD executives to focus on one idea; don't make your task infinitely more difficult by mixing in additional messages.

Case in point: I had spent several weeks with my team working on a presentation. We had worked it, reworked it, and introduced it to everyone, including the CIO. Then I presented it to the executive board. The members listened, and then one person looked at me and said, "There are three different ideas in here; which one do you want us to consider?" I was floored. Needless to say, my story failed because I didn't get whatever it was that I was requesting that day. But it was a great lesson for my team and me. I took the presentation back to them and asked, "How many stories are we telling in this presentation?" As we reviewed it together, we saw it clear as day: there were, in fact, three stories.

The moral: Be sure to keep to just one story line. I recommend you have someone outside the team review the materials, specifically looking at the number of story lines. I know at times it's tempting to add something to the story to make sure it's "comprehensive" or "thorough." Fight the temptation, and keep your stories simple and with a crystal-clear singular focus.

IT'S TEMPTING TO ADD SOMETHING TO THE STORY TO MAKE SURE IT'S "COMPREHENSIVE OR THOROUGH." FIGHT THE TEMPTATION.

C. Drive points with data

Your story outline should be objective. That is to say, your story should be rooted in quantitative and measurable values. I mention this now because you may need to work with others to get the required data for your story. In chapter 1, we discussed the employee who was waking up in the middle of the night to reboot systems. When communicating the effects, he should have been prepared to say, with some precision, how much money was lost or how traffic suffered. The value of the data will determine its placement in the story, but you'd better have it either way. In chapter 3, we'll talk more about metrics and how to present data at the time that is most powerful and advantageous to you.

D. Keep it simple

Consistent with the theme of this book, keep your story outline very simple. Create a story flow that seduces your audience one step at a time: A=B, B=C, C=D, A=D. If you do this right, at each section your executives will be nodding their heads in approval as you sell them on one simple concept, then the next, and so on, until you reach your ultimate conclusion.

E. Ensure your message is clear

Have a child read it. Seriously. If you've outlined the story properly, then anyone who isn't connected with the situation should be able to follow along.

Chapter Summary

Storytelling is not easy, but following a formula is a great way to get started. The Story Analysis approach is just one flow that I've had a lot of success with. It provides five key pieces of information to guide your audience from problem to solution.

A. Current State: Developed from an executive perspective, your current state should take a holistic view and be validated by others before presentation.

B. Future State: Also holistic, the future state should be achievable and sets up the audience for what is to come.

C. Gaps and Barriers: Don't include gaps or barriers that can be resolved at a lower level. Use this time to focus on items that need to be addressed by your current audience.

D. Roadmap: Provide a visual with high-level details.

E. Sustainability: Controls and metrics are required for sustainability. Your controls should be project- and operations-based and take into consideration people, processes, and technology.

Once you've taken the time to build a complete story analysis, you can easily tailor and cut the presentations depending on your audience and time.

In some situations, the full story analysis isn't needed; perhaps this is for a follow-up meeting, or the ideas have already been socialized. As you move your story up the ladder, your presentation time is likely to decrease, along with attention spans. The LeShay Executive 4x4 helps distill your story into the points that really matter to executives. Use the model below to structure your presentation, pulling information from your already-researched story analysis.

Beginning with your problem statement, answer the following questions:

1. What will you do?

2. When will you do it?

3. How much will it cost?

4. What value will it return?
    1. Make money
    2. Save or defer cost
    3. Protect or enhance the brand
    4. Generate compliance

Your audience, especially if it's made up of executives, needs clear information in a story that flows fluidly from one concept to the next. Follow these best practices to stay on track!

- Don't beat around the bush. Be bold and send your message right up front.

- Make sure you only have one story, and keep it simple.

- "Walk" your audience through the story. The storytelling process is a "slow seduction" where A=B, B=C, C=D, and A=D.

- Ensure that your message is clear and that your story flows easily.

Following these guidelines will create an outline that allows your story to have the most impact!

CHAPTER 3

STORY CONTENT DEVELOPMENT
Preview

A rmed with a solid story flow, you now need to develop all your content.

"How will I compile my information into an engaging presentation?"

Through this process, consider the following:

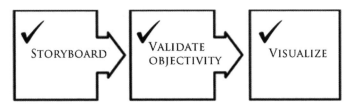

Keys to success:

1. Arrange your content to create the best story, keeping your audience in mind.

   A. Start with a storyboard: solidify and validate your flow and content.
   B. Know your audience: their values and their language.
   C. Don't overcommunicate: less is more.
   D. Keep your message simple: one story, one topic.

2. Provide information, not just data or emotions.

   A. Transcend subjective analysis: metrics fuel your story.
   B. Appendices are your friends: don't sell beyond the close.

3. Illustrate your ideas: a picture is worth a thousand words.

Thoughtful application and visualization of main ideas, supporting information, and measurable value propositions will keep your story clear and focused.

Story Content Development

Now that you've determined there's value to your story and have a general flow, the next step is to develop your content. Aside from the delivery itself, this is the most important step of your story.

1. Arrange Your Content for Your Audience

A. *Start with a storyboard*

In the last chapter, we selected and refined our story outline, our ingredients. Now, we have to figure out how to bake these ingredients into a highly focused and effective story. For most of us, this story takes the form of a presentation, and this book will assume this is the delivery format. However, the process can easily be translated for any medium.

Before starting to fully develop your story, I recommend you start with a storyboard. In this stage, you're collecting your thoughts and the information that will be needed for the presentation. Here's a step-by-step guide on how to create a storyboard:

1. Take blank sheets of paper (in whatever format your presentation will be; typically it will be 8.5 x 11 inches).

2. On each sheet of paper, put the title of the slide. For example, you might put these titles: Contents, Background, Executive Summary, Case for Change, etc.

3. Below the title, in a few words, list the following:

    a) *What is the main purpose of the slide?* For example, "To gain enrollment on the core challenge we're trying to solve."

b) *What are your high-level speaking points?* For example, "Recent use case: symptoms, business response, IT response, root causes."

c) *Any ideas you may have on how to visualize or communicate the story.* For example, "Three columns with overall root causes"

4. Do this for every page in your story.

5. Find a place you can lay these out in sequence, then step back to review the story's message and flow. I like to literally scotch-tape my pages to a wall or large whiteboard.

6. Play with the arrangement and page content until you feel like you've solidified your story's flow.

7. Be sure to include a blank page for your executive summary, which is always the first content slide, and another blank page at the very end for your wrap-up slide. These two slides "bookend" all of your stories and are developed after the story is fully formed.

8. *Critical:* Review your storyboard with someone before you start to develop any visualization or detailed content. Ideally, you "walk" someone from the target audience through the story. If that's not possible, find someone who you trust will provide critical feedback. This achieves two goals:

a) It allows you to walk through the story aloud and see how it feels and sounds to you and your preview audience.

b) It allows for critical feedback and editing from a trusted colleague or target recipient before you invest the labor to develop the entire story.

9. Go over your storyboard enough times until you believe you have the right story flow and content distribution. As you complete versions, continue to edit down your content into succinct ideas.

Below is a sample storyboard page *(illustration 3.1)*. Later in this chapter, we'll revisit this to illustrate the final version of this slide.

Case for Change

Purpose: Gain enrollment from the executive committee on the core issue

Speaking Points:
- ➢ We recently experienced cost pressure and client dissatisfaction because we're only focusing on the symptoms
- ➢ We spent extensive time and money addressing only the symptoms, with poor results
    - ➢ List and illustrate the symptoms and response
- ➢ Punch line: If we don't address the core issues, we'll continue to feel cost pressure and dissatisfaction

- ➢ Note: This slide is a setup for the next, which is a clearly articulated solution that addresses the root causes

Layout: A simple three-column story up top with root causes below.

Illustration 3.1: Storyboard page sample

A short note on the executive summary: I often see people trying to craft their executive summary before they have their entire storyboard. In the same way that you write your introductory paragraph last, your executive summary is the very last story element you create. This is simply pragmatic; you can't develop a summary of your story until you really understand the entire flow. After you complete your storyboard, then you craft your executive summary, which is always your first content slide, a one page "flyover" of the major concepts you're going to present.

With a solid storyboard, you are ready to begin the process of "baking" your story. In doing so, please consider the following:

B. Know Your Audience

Because this book focuses on preparing and telling your stories to executives, we've spent considerable time discussing how to define your story in terms of that specific audience. However, you may have to "socialize" your story to a wide range of people. For example, you may have to first sell your direct leadership team and then go on to meet with your peers or clients, perhaps meet with your staffs, then the senior executive team, etc. While your story remains the same, you need to understand how to adjust your messages for each audience to hit the values dearest to them. For example, in chapter 1 I told of an analyst coming to me and asking for new server hardware because it was failing every night. That was the incorrect message for the executive team. However, this may have been a terrific value point to add when presenting the solution to the staff that had to wake up every night to restart this faulty hardware. This may have had the greatest value resonance with them.

Similarly, this point can be expressed using the previous Temple Grandin story. Since she presented to a panel of ranchers, her values of greater profit, better quality meat, etc., were perfect. If, however, she had presented her story to an animal advocacy group, her more intimate values of treating cattle with humanity would have been far more resounding.

Keep in mind that even within your executive community, you may need to tune your messaging accordingly. The chief financial officer (CFO) may care more about part of your story than the chief information officer (CIO), or the chief marketing officer (CMO), etc. Take time to think about which value propositions will be more effective for your various audience members. If you find yourself presenting to an array of executives, then speak directly to the people to whom your value applies; make eye contact and address that comment to them. This not only creates resonance with your message but also builds a little intimacy.

EXECUTIVES ARE TOP-DOWN THINKERS. MAKE YOUR POINT RIGHT UP FRONT.

C. Don't overcommunicate; less is more

As I've mentioned, executives have very little patience, for there is an army of people constantly asking for their time and attention. You need to be sensitive to this, and your message has to be concise and to the point. You have literally one minute to capture their attention, or they'll move on. As a rule, take whatever you've written or prepared and cut it in half. If you can, try to cut it in half one more time. Yeah, it's difficult; I know you're audibly moaning as you read this. But less is more!

I was a very young executive who managed a huge team of people across multiple departments and three business units.

My executive asked me for a status report. So, I delivered one. She called me on the phone and told me, "Are you kidding me, Marc? I need your status to be two PowerPoint slides."

"But I have a huge team, how can I distill it all down to two slides?" I responded.

She chuckled and told me, "I don't have any idea. But I have to take your status and all my other reports' statuses, and I have to deliver all of that in one PowerPoint presentation. So, if I can do it, you can do it."

That was the end of the call. She was right. I could do it, and I delivered her two crisp, clean slides.

In considering how to distill your story, avoid the following common challenges:

- **"Burying the lead."** Make your point right up front. There's a great tendency to feel compelled to lay foundation, draw out a story, and build to a crescendo. This, again, comes from years of schooling that have created a comfort with this type of storytelling. Fight this urge, and within the first sentence of each of the above areas, tell your executives exactly what you need to tell them. If you feel the need, you can then elaborate. But by taking this approach, you achieve two very important objectives: 1) You tell the executives what you need to before they can get bored and stop paying attention; and 2) if your executives are "sold," you avoid a dialogue that can possibly dissuade them or take your story down a "rabbit hole."

- **Telling them information they already know.** Again, it's natural to want to lay foundation and reiterate the obvious. Don't. Every semester, when I do case studies, I ask the students to assume a role as one of the executives in the case and prepare a summary of the case as if they are that leader delivering a presentation to the executive board. Without exception, early in the semester I receive summaries that say things such as, "XYZ Company was founded in *[insert year]* and today has annual revenue of *[insert dollar value]*," etc. I realize this is a school assignment, but I use it as an illustration because I see it every day in the corporate world. Your executives don't need to be educated on the obvious. Doing so is a very easy way to lose their attention, which is hard enough to get in the first place.

- **Presenting data instead of information.** Do you know the difference between data and information? Data is raw (the "what"); information is interpreted and has meaning (the "so what"). Any sentence you read that invokes the question "So what?" means you need to go back and fine-tune your story. For example, "Third-quarter product releases had significant delays." And— so what? At its essence, your job is to distill complexity into simplicity. Do that with your expertise; tell the executives things they don't know. Provide insights and interpretations of the data to transform it into meaningful information. For example, "Our third-quarter revenue will fall short of our targets because of delays in our product releases."

We added, "Our third-quarter revenue will fall short of our targets." But this catches the executives' attention and, more importantly, provides the context that they need in order to be able to provide the leadership and guidance you're requesting.

TELL THEM THE "SO-WHAT".

As a side note, some of you may be looking at that example and thinking, "Eek, that grammar is terrible." You'd be correct. I'm not suggesting you throw grammar out the window. In fact, proper grammar is very important—as long as it doesn't compromise the story's effectiveness or cause you to add extra words. Again, we as storytellers have to fine-tune and adapt our education to fit our needs.

- **Overloading your audience with information.** Often, people assume that because their executives want details, they have to weigh down their story with a flood of information. This is a surefire way to wind up with a bogged-down story riddled with rabbit holes and distractions. Adding extra information can also create extra story lines and tangents, both of which you want to avoid.

Yes, many executives want details. However, that doesn't mean you need to include all of them. Rather, what you do is summarize your points and then have appendices with the detailed supporting information to present when requested. This works for two reasons:

1. Most executives are top-down thinkers. They want and need you to provide them the top view and then

gradually guide them through the details *as necessary.* This is the key point; don't assume your executives want to dive into every dimension of your story. If they get what you're saying and don't require further detail, move on. In chapter 4, we're going to discuss how to identify verbal and nonverbal cues to know when to advance and when to pause.

2. By organizing your story from the top down, you allow your executives to guide where and when they want to delve into details rather than forcing them to review every piece of information. You allow them to control and adapt their part of the dialogue.

D. Keep it simple

Executives have to focus on a thousand things at the same time and with perpetual distraction. Your job is to simplify the world for them. To find the clear particles amid the chaos. To present them stupidly simple stories. To spoon-feed them small, digestible concepts. To that end, consider the following guidelines:

- **One step at a time.** Be sure that the scope and breadth of your story is achievable. Keep in mind that your audience may not have the same depth of knowledge or comfort in your subject and vision. It's important to step back and look at your story and know when to break it into smaller sections. A lot of people refer to this as a "crawl, walk, run" approach. Understand the appetite for change and make sure your story is broken up so that you can accomplish with a high degree of success what you're selling and then come back and sell the next piece of the story. The original *The Lord of the Rings* was to be one volume of a two-volume set, but the publishers thought the story was too complex and too long, so they decided to break it into three stories so the reader could be taken on this epic journey more easily. Be sure your story can be easily consumed, understood, and achieved.

- **One story; one topic.** The top mistake I see when reviewing stories is that the author commits the cardinal sin of mixing in multiple messages. We touched on this in chapter 2. You have your executives' attention for a very short time. They already have limited focus. The last thing you want is to confuse them by combining stories. More importantly, you don't want to risk shifting their focus away from your primary objective into secondary and tertiary stories. I had a client who was trying to sell the company leadership on an automation project that would increase the speed to market and reduce labor costs significantly. This was a powerful story. But when he created the story, he mixed in the need to reorganize and restructure the vendor contracts. The latter two sub-story lines became "sticking points" for the executives, consuming the majority of the dialogue. As a result, my client never completed his presentation, and his primary story and value were never properly presented and were, therefore, dismissed.

  Most of the time, people don't realize they are doing this. Take the time to ask someone to review your story, specifically looking for this. You get one topic per story. What my client should have done is sold his primary story (automation). Then, as he started to achieve success, he should have gone back with his second story (restructure). Then his next story, if he had one, etc. Sell, achieve success, and build on that success. It's a simple formula.

- **Don't overexplain your points**. Resist the urge to overexplain or overjustify your information. It sounds defensive and raises flags. I once had a remarkably smart and talented woman work for me who consistently explained her analysis to the point that I started to wonder if the reason she kept going on was to rationalize. You don't want that perception. More to the point, you don't want to waste the precious little time and attention you'll get with your executives. If you think the detailed data is necessary, as suggested above, use appendices and have them ready if requested.

- **Use common language.** Executives have big egos, and many will not want to show you that they don't understand something in your story. The reasons for this vary. Some believe it shows weakness; others just don't care enough to inquire; others are embarrassed—there are too many reasons to list. So, consider the following rules:

  1. Never use acronyms without first defining them. Even then, avoid them whenever possible.

  2. Never use industry "lingo," terminology, and buzzwords.

  3. Never use big and fancy words. This is not the time or place to show off your SAT vocabulary. You don't sound smart; you sound pompous. Actions impress; fancy words confuse. More importantly, if the audience cannot understand your story, how and why would it buy into it?

2. Provide Facts, Not Just Data or Emotions

A. *Transcend Subjective Analysis*
Remove the following words from your story vocabulary:

- *Feel*

- *Believe*

- *Think*

- Any other subjective and passive words

Instead, your narration and analysis need to be based on quantifiable and measurable metrics and information, so be *objective*. There are two major benefits to telling an objective story:

1. **It avoids unnecessary distraction**. Metrics and objectivity allow you to avoid debates and discussion that would ultimately distract your audience from your story. Instead of getting into a "he said, she said" debate, your story is rooted in facts.

2. **It earns credibility.** It becomes clear that you've done your research.

There are many kinds of metrics. In many businesses, stories revolve around metrics related to money—that is, costs and revenue. These are great choices but not the only ones. Find metrics that will resonate with your executives. There are hundreds of options. Here are just a few examples: time to completion, uptime, downtime, resource allocation, resource hours, satisfaction, quality, etc. When using a metric, make sure that it's well-defined and measurable.

1) **Definition**. If we have a metric for revenue growth, what does that mean within your context? Is it new revenue? Is it a dollar value? Is it a percentage of current revenue? What is revenue growth in your analysis? Your job is to define the metrics so everyone is using them the same and looking at your analysis through the same lens. For example, you might say, "Revenue growth is defined as the percentage of revenue generated above last year's figure."

2) **Measures**. Define how each metric will be evaluated. Instead of saying "high revenue growth," say "15 percent revenue growth." Instead of saying "project delays," say "project delays by four to six weeks." Building on the previous example, you might say, "Revenue growth is defined as the percentage of revenue generated above last year's figure, where in excess of 15 percent is ideal, 10–15 percent is good, and below 10 percent is undesirable."

Consider the chapter 1 example of the equipment that failed every night. It's not enough to simply say that the downtime resulted in revenue loss. Through research, you may learn that 10 percent of web orders are made between midnight and 5:00 a.m. If the system is down for two hours, and the amount ordered per hour is consistent, you're losing 40 percent of those potential orders. Armed with this information, we can research the average revenue per order and provide executives with a fairly accurate calculation of lost revenue.

Remember to tie your metrics to your audience's value statements. Using the above revenue loss calculation may not be the most impactful if you're presenting to the chief marketing officer. That executive will definitely want to know about the number of people unable to access the website. But the CMO's primary focus may be more related to customer satisfaction and brand reputation. Given this, perhaps a metric that focuses more around sentiment analysis or brand position would resonate more.

B. Appendices are your friends

Too often, I sit in presentations littered and weighed down by heavy analysis and supporting data. This is a surefire way of doubling the size of your presentation and boring your audience. Rather than including all this analysis in your story, create a *separate* appendices document. Why a separate document? We don't want to present unrequested data. If your executives accept your story, why would you want to provide data that can only serve to reverse your positive outcome? It's the proverbial "do not sell past the close." The appendices are there for the next level of discussion to sell your story—but only *if they are needed.*

Let's pretend you walk into a Verizon store, and the salesperson explains the various phone plans, and you say, "I'll take Plan B." The sale is made, but the salesperson then decides to show you the brochure that details the elements of the plan, and you notice you get far more data than you need. Now, you say, "Hold on; I'm not sure. Maybe the less-expensive Plan A is better. I don't know now." You get the idea. As previously explained, less is more. Once your executives say "yes," accept it, and move on before they can change their minds.

3. Illustrate Your Ideas

Looks matter. There's a psychology to creating your story that has to be considered as you develop your content. If your executives look at your story and think, "Wow, that looks nice," you have them. They're already in a mental state of approval. All you have to do now is not lose them in your narration. On the other hand, if their first impression is, "Eww, what's that?"—you have an uphill battle on your hands. I've seen many a great story die before the first word was spoken just because the presentation or document looked bad or amateurish.

I remember working a big consulting job during which I shared an office with one of my client's employees. One day, a friend came into our office and asked me what I was working on. My office mate chimed in and joked, "He's drawing pretty pictures."

I laughed and said, "Executives love pretty pictures. Watch, these are going to get me $10 million of project funding." Fast forward a month. I presented my story and gained the requested $10 million.

Following the meeting, my office mate came up to me and said, "I didn't get what you were doing until I saw your story. But I get it now."

We are highly visual beings. Here are some helpful hints:

- **Use graphics to communicate complex ideas.** It's like the old cliché: "A picture is worth a thousand words." Leverage graphics but be sure to keep them clean and clear. Understand how to edit down your graphics to ensure they enhance the story rather than create distraction. For example:

1) Reduce the number of animations in your presentation. Animations should be used sparingly and only for dramatic effect. Never, never, never have things spin or flash or sparkle or grow. Use one or two animations per presentation for *truly important* content. These should be simple appear, fade-in, or wipe effects. Also, check your template to ensure it doesn't have animations built in. Why would you want to draw attention to the theme and distract from your story?

2) Direct the eye. Use graphics and shapes to direct the reader's eye. Arrows, pointers, and spacing will help achieve this goal. You can see an illustration of this in the sample later in this chapter.

I'VE SEEN MANY A GREAT STORY DIE BEFORE THE FIRST WORD WAS SPOKEN JUST BECAUSE THE PRESENTATION OR DOCUMENT LOOKED UGLY.

---

3) Avoid color combinations like yellow text on black backgrounds or bright red on dark blue. The last thing you want is for your story to be difficult to read.

4) Don't overlap graphics and make the page too busy. Don't make your slide so dense with graphics that it's a kaleidoscope of color and images that overwhelms your audience and sends it into seizures.

- **Select a simple and clean theme/template.** Just as we don't want to clutter the page with wild color combinations and an overwhelming amount of graphics, we want to find a clean and clear template on which we will create our story. For a majority of people, this is already taken care of by their companies that provide corporate-sanctioned templates. For the rest of you, there are literally tens of thousands of free templates you can download and tens of thousands more for purchase. If you need to select a template, take heed:

  1) Color matters. Try to find a template with a nice color palette. I prefer templates that use blue tones because blue mixes and matches very well with a broad spectrum of other colors and also has a lot of hues that look good and print well.

  2) Avoid black backgrounds. Other than toner manufacturers, nobody likes a black background. It's very hard to read, your graphic and font colors are limited, and it prints poorly.

  3) Use a white background. The benefit of a white background is that your graphics will lie better. Many graphics and illustrations that you'll want to include in your story will have white backgrounds. This is due to the graphic format itself and cannot be changed. The challenge with a colored background, even a pale gray, is that when we place these into the presentation or document, we get an undesirable white splotch or square around our image. This isn't a huge deal. Microsoft has a tool to help translate the white to transparent.

Nevertheless, it consumes time and most often yields undesirable results. Why make your job more difficult than it already is? Select a template with a white background and avoid the problem altogether. Plus, graphics and fonts really jump off white backgrounds.

4) Avoid templates with many design elements (graphics, shapes, borders, etc.) already on the page. Many templates look stunning and have beautiful graphics already on the page. It's very tempting to grab one of these. The challenge is twofold:

   a) These graphics often take up considerable space, leaving you little valuable area to create your visual, which is far more important.

   b) These graphics can be distracting and take away from the power of your story.

5) Size matters. Today, many templates are offered in both 4:3 (standard format) and 16:9 (wide screen). If you know the platform on which you'll be delivering your story, select the most appropriate. Below are a few helpful hints to help you identify the right format:

   a) If you are using hard copy only, use whichever format you prefer.

   b) If you are presenting on an overhead projector, use the 4:3 format. Many of the older projectors will squish down your 16:9 presentation, making it look tall and thin like a bad '70s kung fu film.

c) If you are presenting on a TV, which is increasingly common, the 16:9 format works well.

d) If in doubt, use the 4:3 format. This is the safest way to go.

This may seem trivial, but take it from experience: It is not a good feeling to spend all the time to make your story look stunning to just have it look terrible when it really matters. It goes back to my earlier comment: If people like what they see, they subconsciously are in a state of approval. If not, well, you know the rest.

- **Select easy-to-read font styles and sizes**. I realize there are a million font choices, and some are a lot of fun. But be aware of your final venue. If you're presenting to a room of people, recognize that some of your executives may be trying to read a screen as far as fifteen to twenty feet away. Make sure the font style is simple and easy to read and that your text is large enough to read from across the room.

Let's take another look at the earlier storyboard illustration alongside the final slide.

Case for Change

Purpose: Gain enrollment from the executive committee on the core issue

Speaking Points:

- ➤ We recently experienced cost pressure and client dissatisfaction because we're only focusing on the symptoms
- ➤ We spent extensive time and money addressing only the symptoms, with poor results
  - ➤ List and illustrate the symptoms and response
- ➤ Punch line: If we don't address the core issues, we'll continue to feel cost pressure and dissatisfaction

- ➤ Note: This slide is a setup for the next, which is a clearly articulated solution that addresses the root causes

Layout: A simple three-column story up top with root causes below.

Illustration 3.1: Storyboard page sample

Case for Change

Symptoms	Biz Reaction	IT Response
➤ Technology costs are fluid and vague	"We are not competitive in the market: Lower our Tech cost"	➤ Off-site to trim costs
• $45M-$96M		• Target: $4M
➤ Tech debt is high		• Actual: $1.7M
➤ Minimal re-use		➤ Did not address or solve the business problem
➤ Minimal automation		➤ We will be right back here again next year
➤ Duplication of efforts		

Underlining Root Causes

Lack of Trust between the Business and IT

No Unified IT/Biz Strategy	Rising IT Costs	IT Can't Meet Biz Demands

➤ Complex architecture

➤ Legacy cost allocation models

➤ Absence of cost transparency

Business doesn't feel in control

Illustration 3.2: Final page sample

Chapter Summary

Creating the story's content is the most challenging part of the process. Not only do you have to select the key ideas and a delivery format, but you also need to consider your audience, have backup information, and wrap it all up with appealing visuals.

When collecting and editing your story content, remember these points:

1. **Start with a storyboard**. Using this process will allow you to test the flow of your content and move pieces around before you get too far along. It's also a great stage to bring in collaborators and get validation.

2. **Know your audience**. Your story content won't be "one size fits all." Finding ways to relate to the values of your audience will increase engagement and enrollment.

3. **Don't beat around the bush**. Convey what your audience doesn't know. Be up front and answer the "so what." You don't want your audience to have to search through your story to find the key points. When providing information, don't overload your audience with your processes or the analytical data. You can also talk deeper into a point or refer to supporting documents if necessary, but keep your story presentation clean and clear.

4. **Keep your message simple**. Your story should have one topic and flow in a way that leads your audience step-by-step to your conclusion. Overexplaining or including unknown words will only cause your audience to turn its attention away from your story.

Once you have a clear understanding of your story's content, give it more credibility and strength by ensuring that it is objective. The last thing you want is to get derailed by a "he said, she said" debate. When your information is based on metrics and data, you'll have heads nodding in agreement. Of course, your audience may want to know how you gathered the data, but that's what appendices are for.

No matter how solid your story, if it's unappealing to the eye or requires too much work to read and interpret, it will fail. The visual look and feel is just as important as flow, content, and objectivity. When checking the visual appeal of your presentation, consider the following aspects:

- Presentation template, coloring, and font selection

- Borders, design, and background

- Graphics
    - Add to the story
    - Keep them simple
    - Only animate when truly necessary

- Page flow (directing the eye)

A visually inviting presentation generates your first win with the audience. It'll be much easier for it to focus, listen, and watch your professional and sophisticated story presentation.

With your story content ready to go, the next step is to present it to your executives!

CHAPTER 4

STORY DELIVERY
Preview

You've worked hard, and it's finally time to deliver your story.

"How can I tell the best story so that I get what I need from my audience?"

As you prepare for and deliver your story, consider the following:

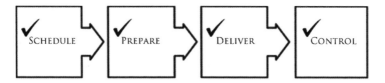

Keys to success:

1. Ensure you schedule your presentation at the most ideal time and with the right audience.

2. Prepare your presentation.

    ▪ Adhere to the ten-slide rule.
    ▪ Have multiple versions of your story.

- Be ready for anything.
- Check your ego at the door.

3. Be a star presenter.

- *Engage* with and connect to your audience.
- Don't create distractions.
- Be bold!

4. Control the room.

- Participation is good; hijacking is bad.
- Read the room so that you know when to change up and when to shut up.

Storytelling takes practice, so spend time rehearsing your delivery.

Story Delivery

First, before you deliver your story, I want you to really challenge yourself. Why do you want or need to present this story? In considering this, ask yourself one key question:

Do I need something specific from my executives?

Your executives are not your therapists. Do not go to them for any of the following reasons:

- To demonstrate your value

- To show how smart you are

- To be heard.

There is only one reason to tell a story to your executives: because you need something from them. It could be financing, resources, advice, or anything of significance that ONLY they can provide.

I was a fairly senior-level executive and had someone from another department set up a meeting with me. We spent an hour together, and at the end I asked, "I'm not sure what you want from me. Are you asking for anything in particular?" He replied, "That's a good question. I think I really just wanted someone in leadership to know what I was thinking." Inside my head, I thought, "This guy just consumed an hour of my double-booked day and didn't actually need anything from me. He will never work on my team." Is that cold and harsh? Absolutely! Is it nearly all executives would think? Absolutely!

Having said this, let's assume that you do need something from your executives. As the old adage goes, "Timing is everything." As we discussed in chapter 2, an incredible story can fail because of bad timing, and a mediocre story can sell because of good timing. As you schedule your story presentation, ask yourself if the timing is right.

1. Scheduling: Timing and Audience

As much as organizations like to believe they move fast, the majority do not. In fact, most organizations run in a series of "hurry up and wait" cycles. Similar to waves hitting the shore, opportunities will appear one after the other, with another one right around the corner. There's not a huge difference in telling your story today or in three weeks. If things are happening that are distracting your audience, hold off for a bit. Wait until the timing is good and then schedule. Like a surfer scanning the horizon, pick the right wave, not just the first that comes along.

Of course, you may not always have the luxury of choosing when to present to your executives, but whenever possible, be tactical about scheduling.

Good Times to Schedule

1. **Carpe Diem.** Crisis breeds opportunity. Following a major failure, a loss of revenue, or any other negative outcome, there is often an opportunity. Consider the country on Sept. 12, 2001. If not for the terrible and tragic events of the day before, do you think the Patriot Act could have been sold to the American public? Maybe, maybe not. But following that horrific event, there's no arguing that the sale was exponentially swifter and easier. I'm not suggesting you hold your story until there's a crisis. Rather,

be aware of what is happening in your business when the opportunity arises; then seize it.

2. **Ride the wave.** Is your company having a big quarter or year, are sales higher than expected, is the company feeling good about growth, etc.? It is always easier to sell during the flows than the ebbs. This seems obvious, and yet I see time and time again people trying to sell upstream against the current of poor business performance and economic conditions.

THERE IS ONLY ONE REASON TO TELL A STORY TO YOUR EXECUTIVES: BECAUSE YOU NEED SOMETHING FROM THEM.

---

3. **Solve the problem.** There is a time to sell your story during ebbs—when you have a solution to the problem. In fact, this may be the very best time to sell your story. However, before you boldly run into the boardroom to announce that you've solved the company's problems, consider for a moment that there are a lot of smart people in that room who are also trying to solve the problem. Before you present your story, make sure you've done your due diligence and check off the following:

a. You know with absolute certainty what the root cause is.

b. You know what the executives are currently considering.

c. Your story is different and, most importantly, *better* than what is being told.

If you've done your homework and believe you have the million-dollar answer, then this is a perfect time to tell it. Cautionary note: Many people fall into the "Superman" complex and try to solve everyone's problems. Make sure you're not overreaching.

4. **Budget season.** I'm cheating here a little bit. This isn't really a matter of good timing as much as an annual rite of passage. You don't have a choice on this one. Each year, you're going to have to endure the ridiculous process of annual forecasting and budgeting. If you haven't yet been through this process, it's often one of the most frustrating times of the year, especially if you are not good at storytelling. For me, budget season was always fun. Why? Because I made sure I told the best story. And the best story always wins. So, I felt great.

5. **Year-end:** Often, organizations or teams will have a budget surplus as they near the end of the fiscal year. Fearful that spending less now will lead to a smaller budget in the future, leaders are often looking for ways to spend. What a great time to tell your story and get the funding you need! They're literally looking to spend.

6. **New blood.** To paraphrase *Apocalypse Now*, I love the smell of new leadership in the morning. New leaders often want to show how they're going to make an impact, demonstrate their value, and differentiate themselves from their predecessors. If you have the opportunity to tell your story to a new leader, don't underestimate the value of schmoozing as you tell the story. Show how the story will spotlight the leader, distinguishing him or her from the predecessor and helping the leader establish value with early contributions to the team.

7. **In the mood**. At any level within an organization, the ability to know and read your audience is critical. If your meeting is scheduled, you don't have a lot of choice in the matter. However, this particular timing recommendation is targeted at the impromptu story. Many times, we have stories that we want to tell and are just waiting for the opportunity. If you see your executive is in a great mood, take advantage of that. Try like hell to get a small slot on the executive's calendar or just go for it when you catch him/her for a quick hallway conversation.

Bad Times to Schedule

1. **Back against the wall**. There are times when you are forced to tell your story. The timing may not be perfect, but good or bad timing, you have no choice. Perhaps your team underperformed, maybe the company as a whole is struggling, or it just so happens there are human resources or legal actions for which the executives need to be made aware. Sometimes you just have to tell your story. This is not ideal, but you have a job to do, and that means telling your story. My advice here is to structure your presentation very simply and carefully, eliminate all subjectivity, be concise, and be prepared to field questions:

    a. What happened?

    b. What is the outcome?

    c. What are you doing to address the situation/issue/problem?

d. What are you doing to ensure it doesn't happen again?

e. What do you need from your executives? As I say at the opening of this chapter and cannot stress enough, if you don't need anything from your executives, why are you telling them your story?

2. **Belt-tightening.** During times of severe cost-cutting, projects targeting only soft value won't sell. Even programs to yield hard value may be difficult to sell, especially in large companies where it is difficult to "move the needle." To be clear, I'm not saying throw up your hands and don't try. Rather, I'm saying this is not an ideal time to sell a story, so be sure yours is targeting cost savings and is very compelling. You may be thinking, "What about revenue-generating stories? Certainly they'd sell." It has been my experience that during times of cost-consciousness, executives have very small appetites for even new revenue-generating ideas. The reason is simple: Typically, they cost money to get off the ground, and the revenue opportunity is in the future and not guaranteed. Some of today's executives tend to be more conservative and shortsighted.

3. **Swing and a miss.** You need to know what is happening in your organization and which problems your leadership team members are passionate about. You may have an incredible story, one that solves a major problem. However, if it's not one of the problems the executive team cares about and is actively focusing on, you may find the leadership members are less than receptive. This presents a huge paradox in today's corporate landscape. On the one hand, so many companies are "building cultures of innovation"; on the other hand, there remains

complacency on doing things the way they've been done in the past and complacency on simply focusing on the problems the company already knows about. These ideologies are at odds. If you are selling innovative stories, then early in your story I recommend you spotlight this paradox; make your executives aware of this dynamic. This will help to shift their psychology and make them more receptive to seeing and considering new problems and solutions.

4. **In a mood**. If we can capitalize on the good mood of our executives, we can also fall victim to their foul mood. Be smart and aware of your audience. If you're scheduled to meet and you can see that your executive is not going to be receptive, either cancel the meeting or present something else. Don't risk having your story fail just because you caught someone on a bad day.

5. **It's raining money**. It sounds counterintuitive, but when things are going exceptionally well, it can be very difficult to sell your story. Success breeds complacency. It's the old "if it ain't broke, don't fix it" mentality that can make it very difficult to introduce new ideas during times of wild success.

6. **Shaking the snow globe**. Massive business transformations such as mergers and acquisitions, wide-scale reorganizations, enterprise-wide programs, etc., create a great deal of uncertainty in an organization. During these times, it's highly recommended that you hold your stories until things settle down. There's only so much change a person or organization can endure at a given time. Unless your story is somehow simplifying the transformation, making the snow globe settle more quickly and efficiently, be patient and wait for calmer times.

Your first audience

Once you've established that the timing is right, you may have the option to choose your audience. Remember what I said earlier about needing something from the executive? In a large organization, you may need a number of business units or leaders to buy into your story and thus have the need to sell to several different groups. The next three sections provide two points of view for choosing to whom you present.

1. *Prey on the weak*

   In this situation, you're finding an audience that needs your help as much as you need its help. Your chance for enrollment will be greater (an easier sell), if you can truly demonstrate the mutual value in your story.

   I once built a new team that was charged with providing a new service to a global media and entertainment company. This was a new team with an associated added cost. The first year's budget was in place, but I had to earn the second and beyond. I had a difficult task ahead of me: I had one year to deliver my story to all the executives across the organization to get them to fund future years.

   Where to start? That's easy: I started with the weakest kid on the block, publishing. Everyone knows that's a dying industry; if anyone needs help, it's publishing. So, I went over and met with the CFO and asked one question: "What is the biggest challenge your business is facing?" He told me, and I left, telling him I'd be back in a week.

   A week later, I returned and told him my story: what my team did, how we operated, and how we were going to solve his problem. He was "cautiously optimistic," as he said. I didn't ask him for money, help, or anything else. I offered him a deal: I'll pay for my team to work on this. If we pull it off and solve your problem, you agree to fund your portion of our team next year and you relay the story to your peers at the Executive Roundtable. He agreed.

Two weeks later, we set up a meeting to demonstrate the solution to the CFO and his team. They went wild. After the meeting, the CFO shook my hand and said, "We have a deal!" And good to his word, he funded us and spread the word, opening new doors throughout the organization.

2. *Dominate the strong*
In this situation, you're finding an audience that will have the most influence, knowing that with their enrollment and support, others will follow. It's similar to a casting agent signing Meryl Streep—other talent will more readily have interest in the project.

With this in mind, and with publishing enrolled in my story, I had to decide where to go next. It was an easy decision. I had to go find the strongest kid on the playground. If I could sell that kid, everyone else would fall in line.

My next stop was TV, by far the largest and most influential business unit. Again, my first meeting was short— "What is your greatest business challenge?" I was told, and I went back to my team. We returned the next week with three ways in which we could help solve TV's problem. All three solutions resonated with the executives, and they welcomed us to their virtual team. This time, my deal with the devil was a little different. "I'll contribute labor to your team to help drive these three initiatives. In exchange, you fund us next year and allow us to leverage the work we do across the organization." If I could leverage the buying power of TV, I could provide massive value to the other business units, making my future sales that much easier.

The executives agreed, and our partnership was sealed with a hug—one TV executive literally hugged me.

3. *Create advocates*
   This approach is great when you need the support of many teams or divisions. Storytelling isn't always one-to-one. When you create a network of advocates, you're getting others excited about your story. If you know that ultimately you need to sell a CFO on your solution, getting internal and external clients to enroll and become vocal advocates ahead of your presentation can greatly influence and sway the CFO.

2. Prepare

You've considered the timing and your approach, and you're ready to present your story. Before you enter the room, there's preparation to be done.

1. **Size matters**. If it's not cut down already, the very first thing you need to do is trim your story to ten slides or less. That's ten slides of content, not including your cover page and summary (so twelve physical slides). Why ten? Executives have ADHD, and I have found

anything longer than ten slides causes them to lose their focus.

I once had a woman on my staff, one of my "rock stars," who was developing a presentation for my boss, the COO/CIO. She came to me with exactly forty-four pages. She handed it to me, and I looked at the pile and said, "There is no way I'm reading this. I won't even look at it until it's ten pages or fewer." She got flustered and told me there's no way she could do that, that all the content was critical. I smiled and just told her she didn't have a choice. I told her the COO/CIO wouldn't even look at the cover page of a forty-four-page presentation. She went off and, over the next two weeks, trimmed and trimmed and trimmed. Finally, she got it to fifteen slides, at which point I helped her trim it down to fewer than ten slides.

Simplifying and shortening your message takes practice. Next time you write something—an e-mail, memo, presentation, or anything—play a game with yourself and see if you can cut it in half. If your e-mail note is two paragraphs, can you make it one without losing any critical content? Can you make your six-slide PowerPoint presentation three? If you put effort into this, you'll find your ability to distill concepts while maintaining their impact will improve tremendously.

2. **Adapt or die**. When presenting to executives, at least one of the following scenarios is incredibly likely.

    a) You'll schedule an hour with your executives, and they'll show up late.

b) They'll tell you they need to leave early.

c) They'll be distracted and come in and out of your meeting, cutting into your time.

Before attending your meeting, you need three copies of your story:

1) A full version.

2) A fifteen-minute version. In advance of your meeting, you should identify what I call the "money slides," the pages that are most critical and are most compelling. Have a smaller version with just the "money slides" that you can deliver in fifteen minutes or less.

IF IT'S NOT ALREADY, THE VERY FIRST THING YOU NEED TO DO IS TRIM YOUR STORY TO 10 SLIDES

---

3) A teaser version (typically one slide). This one slide is intended to pique the executives' interest enough to ensure a follow-up meeting so you can present your story. Use the "teaser" slide if you find your time compressed to less than fifteen minutes. Note: The teaser is not necessarily the executive summary slide. It's the page that will draw the audience in and make it want to hear more. I recall when the movie *Bring it On* was released, the studio put a thirty-second teaser video on the website. It had nothing to do with the major theme of the movie; it was a scene with girls in bikinis washing cars. And it worked! The site was overrun with viewers, and movie ticket sales spiked that week.

3. **Argh!** Do not, do not, do not rely on technology. Before you go to your meeting, you need to print hard copies of your story and have a contingency to account for any technological snafus. Your executives do not want to, and will not, sit there and watch you fiddle with the projector for fifteen minutes. Not only will you lose them, you'll lose that first impression, the psychological advantage we spoke about in chapter 3. If their first impression is "Ugh, this person can't even get the projector working," you are facing an uphill battle for credibility. The moment you have problems, you make a joke, call an audible, and hand out your hard copies or whatever other contingency you designed. This tells your executives, "I'm prepared for anything!"

4. **Check yourself** A graduate-school colleague of mine has a garbage can outside every conference room in his office with a note above it that reads, "Leave your ego and emotions here"—with an arrow pointing to the can. While I'm not sure of his delivery, the sentiment is spot on. Before you walk into a room with an executive or group of executives, you had better check your attitude, ego, assumptions, and emotions at the door. There are enough egos in that room already, and you're there to listen and learn as much as to tell your story. Your executives have a different view of the company and industry than you. They have access to information you don't. They may not know more about your subject or even be as smart as you. Nevertheless, you have to respect that they're privy to information that you don't hold and you should be prepared to listen to them, address their questions and concerns, and do these things without taking offense. You have to face the possibility that your assumptions

may not be totally accurate. In short, "confident humility" goes a long way.

I once judged an entrepreneurial competition at a top-ten business school. These were smart students, the best of the best. At one point, one of my cojudges made a comment, and one student said, "I hear what you're saying, but you're wrong." Yeah, the judge thought the exact same thing you are thinking right now. He was twenty-five, and this was school. So, it was handled firmly but with love. In the corporate world, I hear the same thing said by seasoned leaders all the time. They're smarter and don't say you're wrong, but almost anything that follows the phrase "I hear you but…" is paramount to saying, "You're wrong." Don't think that because you're more experienced than the twenty-five-year-old business-school student that you won't make the same mistake. Believe me, executives pick up on even the slightest amount of ego, defensiveness, and attitude. Be confident but humble.

3. Deliver

It's been a long process. You defined value, outlined your story, developed your content, and prepared for your meeting. All of this hard work culminates in the next hour (or whatever the meeting's length). This is where you actually sell your story. You've put in all the work to be successful, and now you have to deliver. This is your moment to shine! As you tell your story, consider the following:

1. **Breathe**. Don't speak too fast and be sure to leave pauses where people can interject if needed and absorb what you're telling them. Keep in mind that while you know

all of the content, they may not fully understand it, especially within your story context.

2. **Moderate your voice.** This sounds overly obvious, but be sure to emote. Allow your audience to hear what you're saying. That means that you should be aware of your room size, noise, and other factors that could affect people's ability to hear and understand you. Be aware of your voice and moderate it appropriately to the surroundings. And don't speak in a monotone. Mix it up; play with the room.

3. **Check in.** Be sure to check with your audience to ensure it's following along and understanding your story. Again, executives have big egos, and many will not show any indication that they don't understand. So, ask them, "Does this make sense?" or "Are there any questions?"

4. **Read the room.** Even if your executives say they're tracking everything fine, you need to read their body language. Often, people say things very loudly without saying a single word. I've read that up to 93 percent of communication is nonverbal. That means we have to listen to the whole person and not just the person's words. Rather than try to teach this complex topic, take note of the following when telling your story:

   ▪ Is your audience leaning in to you with interest or leaning back with disinterest?

   ▪ Do they look relaxed and comfortable or stiff and uncomfortable?

- Do they look confused and lost, or do they seem engaged with the ideas?

- Are they distracted with other things, or are they focusing on you?

Some people are just not very good at reading subtleties in body language. If you don't feel comfortable doing this, then ask someone to come with you and to help you by providing physical and verbal queues to you. For example, a hand gesture to tell you to speed up or a verbal queue like a clearing of the throat to warn you that people are losing interest. There's no special formula. It just has to be clear between the two of you what the signs are and how you'll respond.

5. **Engage with your audience**. Nobody wants to be lectured to. Engage your executives in the conversation by asking them questions and interacting with them directly, not just as a group. Make eye contact with them. And when you do, try to make a connection with them.

6. **Be bold**. You've worked hard for this moment. Be bold! Get the ugly on the table and have an opinion. It's important that you can demonstrate both sides of the argument. But in the end, you have to take a position and justify it. You have to be willing to put yourself out there, even if it may not be what the executives want to hear. When you go home, whether you've succeeded or failed, you need to be able to look in the mirror and say you did your best. And if you're overly cautious, telling the executives only what they want to hear, you won't feel that way. More importantly, you won't be viewed as a thought leader.

Once, a new client asked me to help out with a strategy. As I engaged with the team, I discovered the client was asking the wrong questions. Now, I could have just done what the client asked and been successful. However, I would not have solved what the client really wanted to solve. I spoke to my client sponsor and explained what I had uncovered during my analysis. He said, "This is great. Would you mind explaining this to my senior VP?" I met with him and showed him my analysis and that we could be successful on our current path. But there was another path I wanted to share with him. He loved it and asked me to develop the broader strategy. Fast forward a month, and I am sitting in a boardroom presenting this new story to the divisional presidents of a major studio. The moral of the story is to be bold because you never know where it will take you.

7. **Anticipate, anticipate, anticipate**. This is perhaps the most difficult of the presentation tips. You want your story to flow so that each piece of information naturally leads to the question that you answer next. You want your narrative to leave them on a cliffhanger, waiting for the next nugget. It's a constant flow, setup, punch line, setup, and punch line. For example, if I tell you that I can save you one hundred dollars off your next phone bill, what will you say next? I'm betting it's asking, "How?"

This seems easy, right? It is if you've been an executive, or around them enough to anticipate where their minds will take them. If you haven't, this can be very difficult. So, ask someone who has been an executive or who knows that audience. When you review your slides, ask that person, "What does this slide make you think. What questions do you have?"

During a recent phone call, a client showed me a short presentation. On the first slide, I asked a question and he responded, "Hmm, that's interesting, I never thought about it that way." It was just me, so no harm. My job was to help him to tune his story so that he would see it "this way" and that he would be prepared when he was in front of his executive team. However, had he not sought out someone such as me, he would have entered that meeting and immediately had his story blown to shreds.

8. **Leave something for the audience to say**. While I want you to anticipate what questions will be asked, I also want you to leave room for audience involvement. Many execs like to contribute, so set them up. Create the space in the presentation where you have a great selling point. For example, I was presenting to a team of executives, and I knew that internal politics had been a growing barrier to their successful execution of their strategy—old-fashioned "turf wars." Knowing this, I listed it first under our potential barriers but didn't provide details. I wanted to lure them in—to get them to ask me what I thought about this issue. They bit. They asked how I planned to approach the stakeholders. It was a setup. I had already met with all the other executives and obtained their enrollment. When I told them, they were ecstatic. Even though they had done absolutely nothing, since they had spotted something that was not in the presentation, they felt like they had contributed to the story. Of course, I

would have told them anyway. But by just holding back a little, I drew them in and got them to feel like they were a part of the presentation and solution. Like all manipulation—yes, this is manipulation—this is a subtle art form to master.

9. **Avoid shiny pennies**. Executives get distracted like a dog chasing a squirrel. Your job is to keep them focused on your story. That means you have to ensure your story doesn't have tangents. As we discussed in chapter 3, your story has to have one focus and one story line. Don't tempt your audience with distraction, complex multipart stories, or shiny pennies.

10. **Dumb it down**. Throughout this book, the idea of keeping things stupidly simple has been a recurring theme. Keep your delivery simple: no jargon or acronyms, no SAT words, one concept at a time, deliver, check in, validate, continue. Your language should be friendly and positive. Your body language should be relaxed yet confident. Your cadence should be rhythmic. The whole experience should feel easy. That's what you want. Stupidly simple and easy.

4. Control the Room

One of the most important but difficult things is guiding your audience on your journey. Often, executives will interrupt, get into sidebar conversations, hijack your meeting, take you into bottomless rabbit holes, or just take you so out of sequence that your story gets muddled. Your job as a storyteller is to keep the audience in line and to control the room.

1. **Keep your audience from jumping around.** Probably the most common way people lose the room is by allowing the audience to bounce around and jump from section to section. One way to avoid this is to not hand out physical copies ahead of time. If you have to, because you are asked for one or because it's your only medium, then just ask right at the top of the presentation for their cooperation while you tell your story. If you receive a question that you cover later in your story, *do not* jump to that page. Rather, provide a cursory answer and let the requestor know that you're going to discuss that in greater detail shortly. Then, when you get there, remind the requestor and fully address the question.

2. **Don't set up rabbit holes.** It doesn't take much to set people off on a tangent. It can be a single word, a bullet on a page, or an entire slide. When you review your story, really take the time to inspect every element. Is each one necessary? Is each one contributing to your story? For example, let's pretend I'm trying to communicate that we need to reorganize the team to increase customer satisfaction. I can write this two ways:

   1. Our customer satisfaction surveys show the number-one complaint among our consumers is the lack of consistency when they call for support. By aligning our support teams with specific products, the customers will receive a more consistent experience.

   2. Our customer satisfaction surveys show the number-one complaint among our consumers is the lack of consistency when they call for support. By aligning our support teams with specific products, the

customers will receive a more consistent experience, and the company will gain greater efficiencies.

Which do you like better? The second one seems more powerful, right? We solve the problem *and* gain efficiencies. While that might be true, the addition of efficiencies now opens all kinds of doors, none of which matter to my core need, which is improving our brand by elevating the customer experience. I now risk being pulled into a dialogue on how we gain efficiencies, including defending each point I make. This could just be a two-minute distraction or it could consume the remainder of our time together. Five words can derail my entire meeting. I want to realign my team to improve customer service. But the conversation I'm now going to get sucked into is whether or not this will gain efficiency. I see this happen in nearly every presentation at which I sit.

To avoid this, you need to train yourself and be disciplined about what you say in your story, to not fall into the trap of wanting to tell too much. Like we've said many times already, less is more.

3. **End sidebar conversations.** We have all been in meetings where sidebar conversations break out. In fact, we've all been guilty of participating in a sidebar or two ourselves. This is a simple fix: Just politely ask you audience to stop. I don't care if you're the janitor presenting to the board of directors; it is well within your control and right to respectfully request their attention and stop sidebar conversations. You can file this under the "be bold" section above. Be humble and respectful, but be bold and take

control of the room. Executives won't respect you if you don't first respect yourself.

4. **Get to a conclusion**. We've spoken about this already. You are telling your story not to entertain but to drive toward clear and quantifiable outcomes. In preparing for your meeting, you should establish goals for yourself that include best-case, moderate-case, and worst-case outcomes. Perhaps you're requesting a project and your best case is the full program with funding, the moderate case is just the first two phases with a smaller budget, and your worst case is a small minimal viable product (MVP) with a limited budget. The only outcome that is unacceptable is deferment to another day, postponement of an answer. Your job is to draw this story to a conclusion, not to meet just to set up another meeting.

For me, the worst-case scenario is always this: They don't buy into the recommended solution, but they recognize and appreciate my thought leadership and contribution. My brand is largely about being a strategic and innovative executive. People pay me for my mind. So, consider that a negative outcome, in terms of getting your story executed, can also be a very positive event as a storyteller. If your executives come away thinking, "He/she was a little off base, but there was some terrific thought there," that's a victory. Executives are always looking for talent and assess it very quickly. If you impress them with your story, whether or not they execute it, they will remember you.

5. **Know when to change up**. No matter how much planning and preparation you do, there's an extemporaneous

nature to all stories. Your audience may be so engaged that you spend extra time on a section, or the room may be fading and you need to speed up. Measuring and adapting your cadence is important. But more than that, your story has to be adaptable. You have to be prepared to switch gears quickly. You may hear something during the meeting that alters your approach.

For example, suppose you have prepared a story that heavily focuses on driving new revenue. During the meeting, you learn that your company is close to acquiring another large organization and that next year is going to be heavily focused on integrating and meeting some serious synergy targets. Your executives have just told you what their focus is and what value they're going to be looking for. At this point, you have three options:

1) Stick with your story, which ultimately leads to failure.

2) Adapt your story to spotlight where and how you will be able to contribute to their synergy targets and integration efforts. If you can really do this, then adapt your story and dynamically incorporate these themes.

3) Abandon your story. This may sound like a bad idea, but it could be the smartest thing. You learned critical new information. It is entirely appropriate to tell your executives that given what you just heard, you don't believe this is the right time for your story, and you thank them for their time. This shows a business maturity that will be appreciated.

6. **Know when to shut up**. *Do not sell beyond the sale.* You've heard this before. Everyone knows this. Yet there seems to be a compulsion to do it anyway. As mentioned in earlier chapters, there's a reason we tell our stories from the top down. One of these reasons is so that we can spoon-feed executives one piece of information at a time—so that each morsel offers a little more detail. As soon as you receive what you want, your job is to shut up and move on. If you suggest to your executives that you're going to reorganize your team and they say OK, *do not* then go into an explanation of why. They haven't asked for it. They said OK. You are done. The only thing you can do now is screw it up and talk them out of it.

I had a client who was in the middle of a large integration project resulting from an acquisition. As part of this, he proposed a restructuring of his team and tried to carve out a new position for himself. He invited me to the meeting to help him tell his story. I presented the case for the overall reorganization, largely rooted in cost-efficiency benefits. During the presentation, I identified a gap and suggested that my client would be a perfect fit. The executive said, "That makes a lot of sense." So, we're done, right? No! My client started to elaborate on why we needed it, and within thirty seconds the executive said, "Wait, now I'm not sure I understand." So, I jumped in and reexplained it, receiving a second approval. We're obviously done now, right? Again, my client spoke up, and predictably, again the executive balked. I wish I was making this up, but this went on for three more rounds until I finally took control of the meeting from my client and ended the dialogue after a final executive approval.

You may be laughing now, but check yourself in your next meeting. I guarantee you do this. You are selling beyond the sale. Perhaps your executives look at your financials and say OK. Your next slide has details on it. I'm going to bet that most of you would still present those and explain them. If so, STOP! Skip that slide. When it pops up on your screen, you simply say, "We covered this already," and you move on.

DO NOT SELL BEYOND THE SALE.

Consider this scenario:

- Your meeting is scheduled for an hour.

- You just reviewed your executive summary and the executive team agrees.

- But you're only five minutes into your presentation.

What do you do? You shut up. You stop right there, thank them for their time, and just end the presentation right then and there. The end.

7. **Bring closure**. There has to be a natural conclusion to your story. Often I see presentations just end on a road-map slide or a funding request. Tell them what you're

going to tell them (executive summary). Tell them (story). Tell them what you just told them (wrap-up). Be sure to close your story with the following:

- A summary of what you just discussed

- Your request—what you want from them, e.g., funding, approval, support, etc.

- Next steps

If you did your job well, there won't be a lot of questions. But obviously, you'll field final questions at the end.

Chapter Summary

What happens during the hour or so you deliver your story will determine whether you are going to get what you need from your executive audience. There are some things that you can't control, but planning ahead and having contingency options will allow you to roll with the punches.

Be aware of current events at your organization. Knowing what situations your executives are facing and their current goals will help you evaluate whether or not that particular time is the time to present your story.

Ask yourself a few questions:

- How is the company doing? Are we in a period of ebb or flow?

- What mood are your executives in?

- Does my story solve a problem that these executives care about right now?

- Can we support another change?

- Who is your first audience?

Once you've determined that the timing and audience are right, make sure you are ready for anything that might happen—technical issues, shortened time, interruptions, new information, etc.

When presenting, constantly assess the room.

- Is my audience engaged?

- Am I checking in with the audience?

- Are we on track, or is this a tangential conversation?

- Have I learned new information that I need to address?

- Have I made the sale? If so, stop right there.

- Am I clearly concluding and summarizing the presentation?

A final thought on delivery: Presenting is not easy. If you are really concerned that your lack of presentation or interpersonal skills will distract from the story, you can ask a strong presenter to step in for you. But the more you practice storytelling, the better you'll become. At a minimum, you want the executives to remember you for your thought leadership and contributions. That only happens when you get up and deliver your story.

POSTSCRIPT

I n the introduction, I said, "My goal with this book is not only
to help you learn how to do this [develop and tell stories],
but also to provide you with the tools to make you highly proficient and skilled in the process." I sincerely hope I have lived
up to that commitment.

As I mentioned, I never thought of myself as a good writer,
which forced me to rely on PowerPoint presentations. When I
started this process, I had no idea of how to design or create
stunning visuals. To teach myself, I collected anything that I saw
or read that made me take notice, even if I couldn't put my fin-
ger on why it caught my eye. I created a file folder and stored
dozens of these documents, cards, and literally anything else that
I liked.

As I prepared to create my visual story, I took out the folder
and spread out all these materials around my dining room table.
I thought about what it was that I was trying to convey and whether any of these artifacts would provide a good way to illustrate
the concepts. I always found a couple that worked, and I created
derivatives of these.

Over time, I started to develop my own aesthetic and relied on my samples folder less and less. Eventually, I found I didn't need it any longer because I could imagine the story and craft terrific visuals.

To this date, I still can't resist grabbing something that impresses me and looking at it, dissecting it, and taking elements of it.

Armed with the formula, illustrations, and many tips presented in this book, your journey starts now. Moving up in an organization means demonstrating thought leadership and effective communication. Storytelling is not a luxury; it's a necessary skill.

In closing, thank you for reading my book. I hope you found it valuable and enjoyable.

The best story wins!